A Tribute to Straddling Hope

A Journey between Destiny's Inflections

Gaurav CJK

SPI PUBLICATIONS

This is a work of fiction. Names, characters, organisations, places, events, and incidents are either products of the author's imagination or are used fictitiously. Any resemblance to actual persons, living or dead, or actual events is purely coincidental. Mentions to use and connection with Indian Scriptures is completely fictional, no intentions to harm the sentiments of people were done. Author highly respects the cultural values, traditions and customs of the people and the society.

Published by **SPI Publications**, www.spipublications.in

SPI, the **SPI logo**, and **Split Poetry India** are trademarks of **SPI Publications**, or its affiliates.

ISBN-13: 978-81-952930-3-2
ISBN-10: 81-952930-3-2

First Edition 2021

SPI Publications

Corporate & Editorial Office
117/2, Sector 37, Khandsa Road,
Gurgaon, Haryana 122 001
Phone: +91 124 428 0743
Email: contact@spipublications.in
Website: www.spipublications.in

ACKNOWLEDGEMENT

I'm pretty sure that you must have witnessed various inflection points in your life; some in timelines, some in every breath. The extreme highs and lows, from optimism to pessimism, from 'I love' to 'I hate' etc. However, the more I've observed myself and my surroundings, what amazes me is the correlation of hope with every single one of these points.

Hope, or the lack of it too, are deeply-rooted in our experiences and we often don't give it due credit. Well, here I am then! This book is raw, personal and an ode to various situations highlighting the presence/absence of hope. This book encompasses 20 of my poems, that are solely for you to witness and maybe even relive moments of hope; within, and at the edges of the spectrum. I hope you are buckled up as you're about to step onto an emotional roller-coaster ride.

Before we begin, a massive shoutout to all of you to buy this book in tumultuous times for written content. A big thank you to writing communities namely Eunoia Prompts, Heart of Quill, Poet Connection and Split Poetry India for muses in the form of prompts that inspired me to write some of these pieces. A big thank you to such kind and exquisite wordsmiths for their everlasting support on Instagram and various other platforms. Them, along with such encouraging friends have always helped me stay zealous about writing. And finally, the woman who has been the pillar of support throughout my journey, my Mom!

Follow me on Instagram: @a_dreamer_in_the_making

HERE WE GO!!!!

Table of Contents

Search For Autumn

The leaves are straddled up on the tree

No flinch, no flow

Dry and lifeless they lie

Waiting to rejuvenate, but time is slow

The tree wants to shed

But right now, it's searching for wind instead

Lonely, it tries to stand

But deep within, it's in search of new land

Then came a gust

A gust it so searched for

Something to bow down weight

Something that arrived before it was too late

The end is finally here

To the search for autumn

The dead leaves that once demoted beauty

Now lie right at the bottom

Now the tree can breathe

And hope for green

Now the joy for dawn

Can evidently be seen

The Proposal

Something weird had happened once

A different feel in the eye contact

Earlier, she would shy away

But that night, she kept it intact

I knew about my feelings though

Plus I had a feeling at the back of my head,

That there must be something between us,

Even if its only an ocean!

But when I felt like swimming in it,

So did she!

The theory of soulmates resonated within my moonstruck self

My intuition suggested that she was in the same drought as me

That's when I thought,

That I got my glint

It's funny how this aubade of mine

May have reached its end, courtesy of a possible hint

A Tribute to Straddling Hope

But hey, the end isn't near

I still had to articulate

Whether I'd cherish or regret this forever

I left it on fate

The next day, I planned a dinner

Luckily, it wasn't so awkward

However, I got heavy jitters

Thinking about the way forward

Took her to a restaurant

Chit-chatted a lot

"What's gonna happen next?"

To myself, I thought

Just before we left for home

I took her past the shore

As we walked through a path with flowers and lights

My heartbeat became more hardcore

A Tribute to Straddling Hope

A few red balloons encompassed the speaker

From which played our favorite song

Then I recited my lines

An those lasted really long

When is love ever enough?

But I hoped that for her, this wasn't rough

I did feel I got too cringe at some point with the lines

But just when I was scared that what we had may perish

She cried and said, "This is the proposal I dreamt of"

And to this day, these are the words I continue to cherish

Yin & Yan

He's spontaneous

She's steady

When he's all pumped

She isn't ready

She's vivacious about planning

While his capacity to plan is ephemeral

She didn't see slowness as prosaic

While he prefers to live a life that's peripheral

They quarrel

Agreement between them is arduous

However, they had the capacity to see

That eventually, what would happen was just meant to be

Eventually they'd be at peace

A Tribute to Straddling Hope

Because they could accept, with no ego at all

They believed in God for the best to happen

And the best always stood tall

Overthinking

So here we are

Stagnant from the day before

There's murk and I'm blindfolded

But I wouldn't let a star knock my door

No doubt I'm jaunty

But I let sadness garble

It's insatiable appetite to straddle

Has made me a pregnable marble

I do find solutions

But mostly I find the founts of issues

From sprawling to jittering

I feel like I've run out of tissues

My eyes are open

But I'm blurred to reality

Reality becomes my semblance

To a world scarce from sanctity

A Tribute to Straddling Hope

I often cage myself

Into thinking,"When will I be free?"

So I'll just try to get a good night's sleep

Or maybe not? Let's see

Time Flies

Time flies, people pass by

One may stay

And a hundred may go a million miles away

But the one who is by your side

Will hold back their tears and smile to you

Whenever you've cried

Let time do the talking

While you keep walking

Never doubt yourself for what happened before

It rejuvenates your future, so look forward to what's in store

Life is like a ride

You never know what's next

But keep in mind

The journey's always the best.

Billie Jean is Not My Lover

Billie Jean is not my lover

Just a fragment of my brain

So many nights I would drain

Thinking about our first encounter

Hypothetical to say the least

Different scenarios enjoying their banter

She was an image

Somehow I felt I was meant to meet her

After all, she was among those I never saw

Yet in my mind, she had to occur

Then at a party one day,

I don't know if it was for the better,

But I finally met her

We danced, we sang, we drank

Then came intimate moments, where our hearts sank

A Tribute to Straddling Hope

But,

To this day

I say,

That Billie Jean is not my lover

Wish her memories donned an opaque cover

A Conundrum within my dreams became an abject experience that I regret

But to our misery

She cannot seem to forget

I guess we were at 2 ends of fate

But I don't know how else to articulate

I know that there were nights to savor

But regardless, Billie Jean is not my lover

The Dichotomy

As I saw the words on the mirror

It remained stagnant, easy to perish

But as I saw them in your eyes

It became a poetry, for me to cherish

That's the power you had

That stopped me from being abrasive, precarious

You blessed me

With sanctity and rectitude, in moments that are various

I nimble

I flinch

But I become calm

As you approach me, inch by inch

But I still get worried

I'm still concerned

Your reluctance to articulate

Is quite discerned

A Tribute to Straddling Hope

Why is it that you take care of me

And I can't reciprocate?

Why is it that you're so percolated

And show your life as perpetually ornate?

To make your darkness ephemeral

I would light the candle

I would carry the abject weight

That you find hard to handle

Tell me if you cannot hit the right note

Mellifluous isn't what life is always

I'll be by your side, whether you laugh or bawl

And regardless of whether you have good or bad days

Life Goes On

The heart does look filled

But there's space for more

Earlier, I felt that the ocean was mine

But now, I'm scared to go past the shore

There was sincerity

But probably no stable roadway

Saw a scarcity of stars at night

And no sun in the day

What is love that just meets you at your destination?

Love is what follows you in your journey

I guess our journeys differed

From what we preferred

And that's why my treasure witnessed poverty

A Tribute to Straddling Hope

But life goes on

May the breeze always bring spring to your fortune

Hopefully nothing changes

And I shall meet you soon

Maybe our joy lies at the 2 ends of the street

And we may never hold hands

But there isn't any need to retaliate

This where reality stands

Every moment, you shall dance

Every moment, you shall embrace

I'll always pray

That whoever you choose brings a smile to your face

All about Hope

The words just flow

And time's everything but slow

When you cross my mind

These are moments of serendipity

Because life gets more clarity

When you cross my mind

About my thoughts

I don't know how you'll feel

Whether you'll flinch in disarray

Or actually show some zeal

I don't know what the future holds

Whether for us, you see any scope

But I'll wait for your answer

After all, it's all about hope

It's all about hope

Empty Spaces

Empty spaces

The shelter of our romance

A record player, a little dance

It was just one of those last minute plans

The way we looked at each other

Eye to eye, sighting each other's feelings

Didn't speak much

Actually, we didn't need to

It were just the voices of our souls

That we paid heed to

The perfect climax

Was the morning sunrise

As we got up to see each other once more

We saw serendipity in disguise

A Tribute to Straddling Hope

A smile on my face

As I looked at her just before I closed the door

With hope for more

For what's next in store

Sunshine

The sun has risen again

Yet we don't let our shadow free

The sky has no limit, but here we are straddled

Unable to trawl beyond the bottom of the sea

The stars gaze at night

Trying to make our world seem exclusive

But it departs answerable to the moon

As catching our attention is elusive

We created our drought

When the entire ocean is ours

While we should heal ourselves

We somehow create new scars

Open the curtains and sleep

And look forward to what's next in line

Because our shade can only be a resistance

But not a barrier for the recurring sunshine

Between My Mirror and I

"Do I know you?

You've changed from what I saw earlier.

I've suddenly started to cherish watching you.

I can now egg myself glow within you.

I can egg you seeking light rather than shadow.

I can enable you to shake your leg, sing, unabashedly make comical faces etc.

Finally, I have started to adore you.

Your altered confident and carefree persona has finally struck my soul.

Stay like this and don't change.

After all,

My personality reflects upon that of yours."

Long Lost

Her eyes had the zeal

For every pain to heal

Promises, there were various

But.............

They all eventually became precarious

Earlier the heart was pounding

But now it's been pounded

Times have become poignant

Gone were days when her presence left me astounded

Earlier the wind had a redolence

One of its kind!

But it's ferocity

Left me with our shadows behind

She once said, "You have the spark"

But it faded, faded and eventually vanished

And now, I have nothing to brighten the dark

And When our Eyes Meet Again

And when our eyes would meet again,

I hope that our thoughts, feelings and senses are in sync

And when our eyes would meet again,

I pray, that the moment is worth all the ink

And when our eyes would meet again

I promise, I won't blink

Find Me

I am the gust of wind brushing off your hair,

Detect me from my essence

Many are clueless of my existence

And seldom catch hold of my presence

I have been asked by the skies to appear several times

But I often leave poignant

Didn't know that a pile of travelling dust

Has made my charm distant

The tiny shabby particles are often witnessed

Their recent abundance has left the blue sky unnoticed

Within y'all, I want to propagate

But how do I reach?

There is no vision to navigate

A Tribute to Straddling Hope

Try seeking me again and again

I'm still nowhere out of reach

The reverberation of my voice is suffocated in the filth

Just try harder to leach

Remove your glasses and clear the fog

And look outside exuberant

Who knows that I can still be found

In a world, that might again seem vibrant?

It All Started With

An instagram story

A hilarious pun that made me cry

Even though we barely spoke back in the day

I just had to reply

What followed were a few emojis

Surprising that you didn't find my message extraneous

Then you gave me some context to the joke

And that made it much more hilarious

I was about to sleep

And I reckoned you too had to sprawl

But then you initiated conversation on life post school

And it definitely was a start, even though it was small

A Tribute to Straddling Hope

We spoke the next day, and the day after

Then what followed were snaps

What was so funny was that you asked me if i was still with that girl
from the past

With so much optimism, seemed like you were the only one who
thought it would last

Life is indeed vagrant

Never ever did I think we'd share a few thoughts

It seemed like we had to be bonded somehow

And destiny was desperate to connect the dots

A look past with a grin was all before

Now, its longing for chats and zoom calls too

Saw you on video after so long, with a new hair color and diffcrent
specs

Even with the change, all my mates would still go head over heels
for you

I became an open book

And you too shared quite a bit

We spoke about our struggles, friends, crushes etc

And I admire you for staying strong after so much shit

A Tribute to Straddling Hope

Tomorrow, I'll finally see you in person

I hope its a crackerjack of a hangout

And I hope that you feel the same way too

We still have so much to share and talk about

Who knows what will happen?

It may be the same as it has always been

But what excites me is that finally

There will be no screen in between

Alpha Male

Why are you so weak and pale?

You're the hero, the alpha male

But each time you cry

All those traits seem a lie

You are the messiah

You have the power to trawl

But its utterly disgraceful

Seeing you bawl

You don't need anyone

Yet why do you long for ears

Vulnerability isn't your forte

You're the tissue to your own tears

And the sole warrior of your fears

A Tribute to Straddling Hope

Why is it that you're so overt

You must be perpetually covert

Is it that you want to tell people how you feel?

But then the macho feels reel

Now if you desire to stay impregnable or not

Its definitely not your call

You must be unhindered to pain

Get over with it

Once and for all

The Cage

It remained closed

It resisted nature's high leverage

I felt it was trivial to look out

I was content living in the cage

I got claustrophobic

I was straddled in thinking if the weather had changed or not

Yet I was reluctant and I don't know why

Maybe I had gotten so monotonous, that I lost the motivation to try

But one day, my source of air became dysfunctional

And desperation confronted me

Perhaps it was high time

That I open the ledge and see

OH!!! The zephyr that I felt on my face

The intrinsic pit stop to a vagrant race

A Tribute to Straddling Hope

The lachrymal and rainbow juxtaposed

Made me wonder that until now

Why was this window closed??

The window to emotions

I was in awe of my action's simplicity

And the outcome as well

I finally felt free!

The spark from the bonfire

The light that the stars constitute

My desires and thoughts inculcated their worth

As they were earlier in destitute

Now I had no reason to panic

Since then, I left the open ledge static

I sensed peace and zeal encapsulating me

While grasping a breath that is indeed more organic

Droplets

There was hope for heavy showers

But what plopped were petty droplets

I was hoping to have found the right track

But now I doubt my instincts

What is love anymore

Just a blanket to comfort my fears

Droplets from rain are sporadic

All that's pouring are tears

Our love is like the verses of the poem

Sadly, you wrote it for others

And I wrote it for you

I thought I found a part of my heart

But you aggravated the rupture

For me, it was nature

But for you, stature

A Tribute to Straddling Hope

It was okay to be single

Why did you succumb to peer pressure?

I was a fool to even think that your love was genuine

Spouting conjecture about us became your favorite leisure

A few cheesy poems of yours on Instagram

That you were too "busy" to write

And I was perpetually left jovial by the saccharine words

Which prompted me to hug you tight

Nevertheless, we had our moments

Those were the best

I'd cherish them always

And will try to ostracize the rest

Now I'm just straddled

Whether to drive ahead

Or park instead?

Your semblance spread and fogged my way

How I wish you didn't leave me like this

In a state of constant disarray

The Road Ahead

Life's a long road

A highway with innumerable exits

Don't know which one seems rights

Some lead to unhindered peace, while others to blitz

I am a traveller

I've been on the road for quite a while

Seen many speed on the way

I just got a moment to glance at them and smile

Sometimes I know the directions

But I do occasionally lose my way

Although the wanderlust keeps me going

The desire to go further, sparkles the inky day

There have been quite a few speed bumps

And there may be more in time

But they give us a moment to slow down

After all, pressing the brakes isn't a crime

A Tribute to Straddling Hope

I was taught to never rush

To never aim to overtake all

All our cars are meant for different roads

Where each of us can stand tall

I'm clueless about the finish line

To be honest, I'm not even bothered

I want to enjoy the drive instead

I'm sure there's a path where I'm meant to go

Until then, I'll just enjoy the road ahead

www.ingramcontent.com/pod-product-compliance
Lightning Source LLC
LaVergne TN
LVHW041442170726

843492LV00008B/2761